ONE HOUR

with

THE BIBLE

NASHVILLE, TENNESSEE

ISBN-13: 978-1-5359-4043-6

Printed in China
1 2 3 4 5 22 21 20 19
RRD

CONTENTS

Genesis 1–2:3 1

Genesis 2:15–3:24 3

Genesis 12:1-3 7

Genesis 17:1-8 7

Exodus 3:1-15 8

Exodus 12:21-23,29-32 10

Exodus 19:3-6 11

Exodus 20:1-17 11

Psalm 78:1-8,17-39 13

Joshua 1:1-9 16

Judges 2:6-19 17

1 Samuel 7:15–8:8 18

1 Samuel 16:1B,6-13A 19

2 Samuel 7:8-16 20

2 Chronicles 36:15-23 21

Jeremiah 29:4-7,10-14 22

Jeremiah 31:31-34 23

Isaiah 52:13–53:12 24

Luke 1:26-35,38 26

Luke 2:1-7 27

Mark 1:9-20 28

Matthew 4:23-24 29

Matthew 5:3-12 29

Matthew 6:9-13 30

Matthew 16:13-21 31

Matthew 22:35-40 32

Matthew 26:20-30 32

Luke 22:39-48 33

John 18:29–19:16 34

Luke 23:32-56 36

Luke 24:1-12,36-53 38

Acts 2 40

Romans 3:21-26 44

Romans 10:8B-13 44

Ephesians 2:1-10,13-22 45

Revelation 21:1-8 46

Revelation 22:16-17,20-21 . . 47

INTRODUCTION TO THE CHRISTIAN STANDARD BIBLE®

The Bible is God's revelation to humanity. It is our only source for completely reliable information about God, what happens when we die, and where history is headed. The Bible does these things because it is God's inspired Word, inerrant in the original manuscripts. Bible translation brings God's Word from the ancient languages (Hebrew, Greek, and Aramaic) into today's world. In dependence on God's Spirit to accomplish this sacred task, the CSB Translation Oversight Committee and Holman Bible Publishers present the Christian Standard Bible.

TEXTUAL BASE OF THE CSB

The textual base for the New Testament (NT) is the Nestle-Aland Novum Testamentum Graece, 28th edition, and the United Bible Societies' Greek New Testament, 5th corrected edition. The text for the Old Testament (OT) is the Biblia Hebraica Stuttgartensia, 5th edition.

GOALS OF THIS TRANSLATION

- Provide English-speaking people worldwide with an accurate translation in contemporary English.
- Provide an accurate translation for personal study, sermon preparation, private devotions, and memorization.
- Provide a text that is clear and understandable, suitable for public reading, and shareable so that all may access its life-giving message.
- Affirm the authority of Scripture and champion its absolute truth against skeptical viewpoints.

TRANSLATION PHILOSOPHY OF
THE CHRISTIAN STANDARD BIBLE

Most discussions of Bible translations speak of two opposite approaches: formal equivalence and dynamic equivalence. However, Bible translations cannot be neatly sorted into these categories. Optimal equivalence capitalizes on the strengths of both approaches.

Optimal equivalence balances contemporary English readability with linguistic precision to the original languages. In the many places throughout the Bible where a word-for-word rendering is understandable, a literal translation is used. When a word-for-word rendering might obscure the meaning for a modern audience, a more dynamic translation is used. This process assures that both the words and the thoughts contained in the original text are conveyed accurately for today's readers. The Christian Standard Bible places equal value on fidelity to the original and readability for a modern audience, resulting in a translation that achieves both goals.

HISTORY OF THE CSB

Holman Bible Publishers assembled an interdenominational team of one hundred scholars, editors, stylists, and proofreaders, all of whom were committed to biblical inerrancy. Working from the original languages, the translation team edited and polished the manuscript, which was first published as the Holman Christian Standard Bible in 2004.

A standing committee maintained the translation, while also seeking ways to improve both readability and accuracy. As with the original translation, the committee that prepared this revision, renamed the Christian Standard Bible, is international and interdenominational, comprising evangelical scholars who honor the inspiration and authority of God's written Word.

In the beginning, the all-powerful, personal God created the universe. This God created human beings in his image to live joyfully in his presence, in humble submission to his gracious authority. But all of us have rebelled against God and, in consequence, must suffer the punishment of our rebellion: physical death and the wrath of God.

Thankfully, God initiated a rescue plan, which began with his choosing the nation of Israel to display his glory in a fallen world. The Bible describes how God acted mightily on Israel's behalf, rescuing his people from slavery and then giving them his holy law. But God's people — like all of us — failed to rightly reflect the glory of God.

Then, in the fullness of time, in the person of Jesus Christ, God himself came to renew the world and restore his people. Jesus perfectly obeyed the law given to Israel. Though innocent, he suffered the consequences of human rebellion by his death on a cross. But three days later, God raised him from the dead.

Now the Church of Jesus Christ has been commissioned by God to take the news of Christ's work to the world. Empowered by God's Spirit, the Church calls all people everywhere to repent of sin and to trust in Christ alone for our forgiveness. Repentance and faith restores our relationship with God and results in a life of ongoing transformation.

The Bible promises that Jesus Christ will return to this earth as the conquering King. Only those who live in repentant faith in Christ will escape God's judgment and live joyfully in God's presence for all eternity. God's message is the same to all of us: repent and believe, before it is too late. Confess with your mouth that Jesus is Lord and believe in your heart that God raised him from the dead, and you will be saved.

The Bible begins with the story of how God created the world and made human beings in his image, and then how they rebelled against him and brought sin and death into the world.

GENESIS 1–2:3

In the beginning God created the heavens and the earth.

Now the earth was formless and empty, darkness covered the surface of the watery depths, and the Spirit of God was hovering over the surface of the waters. Then God said, "Let there be light," and there was light. God saw that the light was good, and God separated the light from the darkness. God called the light "day," and the darkness he called "night." There was an evening, and there was a morning: one day.

Then God said, "Let there be an expanse between the waters, separating water from water." So God made the expanse and separated the water under the expanse from the water above the expanse. And it was so. God called the expanse "sky." Evening came and then morning: the second day.

Then God said, "Let the water under the sky be gathered into one place, and let the dry land appear." And it was so. God called the dry land "earth," and the gathering of the water he called "seas." And God saw that it was good. Then God said, "Let the earth produce vegetation: seed-bearing plants and fruit trees on the earth bearing fruit with seed in it according to their kinds." And it was so. The earth produced vegetation: seed-bearing plants according to their kinds and trees bearing fruit with seed in it according to their kinds. And God saw that it was good. Evening came and then morning: the third day.

Then God said, "Let there be lights in the expanse of the sky to separate the day from the night. They will serve as signs for seasons and for days and years. They will be lights in the expanse of the sky to provide light on the earth." And it was so. God made the two great lights—the greater light to rule over the day and the lesser light to rule over the night—as well as the stars. God placed them in the expanse of the sky to provide light on the earth, to rule the day and the night, and to separate light from darkness. And God saw that it was good. Evening came and then morning: the fourth day.

Then God said, "Let the water swarm with living creatures, and let birds fly above the earth across the expanse of the sky." So God created the large sea-creatures and every living creature that moves and swarms in the water, according to their kinds. He also created every winged creature according to its kind. And God saw that it was good. God blessed them: "Be fruitful, multiply, and fill the waters of the seas, and let the birds multiply on the earth." Evening came and then morning: the fifth day.

Then God said, "Let the earth produce living creatures according to their kinds: livestock, creatures that crawl, and the wildlife of the earth according to their kinds." And it was so. So God made the wildlife of the earth according to their kinds, the livestock according to their kinds, and all the creatures that crawl on the ground according to their kinds. And God saw that it was good.

Then God said, "Let us make man in our image, according to our likeness. They will rule the fish of the sea, the birds of the sky, the livestock, the whole earth, and the creatures that crawl on the earth."

So God created man in his own image;
he created him in the image of God;
he created them male and female.

God blessed them, and God said to them, "Be fruitful, multiply, fill the earth, and subdue it. Rule the fish of the sea, the birds of the sky, and every creature that crawls on the earth." God also said, "Look, I have given you every seed-bearing plant on the surface of the entire earth and every tree whose fruit contains seed. This will be food for you, for all the wildlife of the earth, for every bird of the sky, and for every creature that crawls on the earth—everything having the breath of life in it—I have given every green plant for food." And it was so. God saw all that he had made, and it was very good indeed. Evening came and then morning: the sixth day.

So the heavens and the earth and everything in them were completed. On the seventh day God had completed his work that he had done, and he rested on the seventh day from all his work that he had done. God blessed the seventh day and declared it holy, for on it he rested from all his work of creation.

GENESIS 2:15–3:24

The LORD God took the man and placed him in the garden of Eden to work it and watch over it. And the LORD God commanded the man, "You are free to eat from any tree of the garden, but you must not eat from the tree of the knowledge of good and evil, for on the day you eat from it, you will certainly die." Then the LORD God said, "It is not good for the man to be alone. I will make a helper corresponding to him." The LORD God formed out of the ground every wild animal and every bird of the sky, and brought each to the man to see what he would call it. And whatever the man called a living creature, that was its name. The man gave names to all the livestock, to the birds of the sky, and to every wild animal; but for the man no helper was found corresponding to him. So the LORD God caused a deep sleep to come over the man, and he slept. God took one of his ribs and closed the flesh at that place. Then the LORD God made the rib he had taken from the man into a woman and brought her to the man. And the man said:

> This one, at last, is bone of my bone
> and flesh of my flesh;
> this one will be called "woman,"
> for she was taken from man.

This is why a man leaves his father and mother and bonds with his wife, and they become one flesh. Both the man and his wife were naked, yet felt no shame.

Now the serpent was the most cunning of all the wild animals that the LORD God had made. He said to the woman, "Did God really say, 'You can't eat from any tree in the garden'?"

The woman said to the serpent, "We may eat the fruit from the trees in the garden. But about the fruit of the tree in the middle of the garden, God said, 'You must not eat it or touch it, or you will die.'"

"No! You will not die," the serpent said to the woman. "In fact, God knows that when you eat it your eyes will be opened and you will be like God, knowing good and evil." The woman saw that the tree was good for food and delightful to look at, and that it was desirable for obtaining wisdom. So she took some of its fruit and ate it; she also gave some to her husband, who was with her, and he ate it. Then the eyes of both of them were opened, and they knew they were naked; so they sewed fig leaves together and made coverings for themselves.

Then the man and his wife heard the sound of the LORD God walking in the garden at the time of the evening breeze, and they hid from the LORD God among the trees of the garden. So the LORD God called out to the man and said to him, "Where are you?"

And he said, "I heard you in the garden, and I was afraid because I was naked, so I hid."

Then he asked, "Who told you that you were naked? Did you eat from the tree that I commanded you not to eat from?"

The man replied, "The woman you gave to be with me—she gave me some fruit from the tree, and I ate."

So the LORD God asked the woman, "What is this you have done?"

And the woman said, "The serpent deceived me, and I ate."

So the LORD God said to the serpent:

Because you have done this,
you are cursed more than any livestock
and more than any wild animal.
You will move on your belly
and eat dust all the days of your life.
I will put hostility between you and the woman,
and between your offspring and her offspring.
He will strike your head,
and you will strike his heel.

He said to the woman:

> I will intensify your labor pains;
> you will bear children with painful effort.
> Your desire will be for your husband,
> yet he will rule over you.

And he said to the man, "Because you listened to your wife and ate from the tree about which I commanded you, 'Do not eat from it':

> The ground is cursed because of you.
> You will eat from it by means of painful labor
> all the days of your life.
> It will produce thorns and thistles for you,
> and you will eat the plants of the field.
> You will eat bread by the sweat of your brow
> until you return to the ground,
> since you were taken from it.
> For you are dust,
> and you will return to dust."

The man named his wife Eve because she was the mother of all the living. The Lord God made clothing from skins for the man and his wife, and he clothed them.

The Lord God said, "Since the man has become like one of us, knowing good and evil, he must not reach out, take from the tree of life, eat, and live forever." So the Lord God sent him away from the garden of Eden to work the ground from which he was taken. He drove the man out and stationed the cherubim and the flaming, whirling sword east of the garden of Eden to guard the way to the tree of life.

After the first humans rebelled against God, sin and death spread throughout the world with terrible consequences. But God initiated a rescue plan, centered upon a man he called to faith and obedience.

GENESIS 12:1-3

The LORD said to Abram:
Go out from your land,
your relatives,
and your father's house
to the land that I will show you.
I will make you into a great nation,
I will bless you,
I will make your name great,
and you will be a blessing.
I will bless those who bless you,
I will curse anyone who treats
   you with contempt,
and all the peoples on earth
will be blessed through you.

GENESIS 17:1-8

When Abram was ninety-nine years old, the LORD appeared to him, saying, "I am God Almighty. Live in my presence and be blameless. I will set up my covenant between me and you, and I will multiply you greatly."

Then Abram fell facedown and God spoke with him: "As for me, here is my covenant with you: You will become the father of many nations. Your name will no longer be

Abram; your name will be Abraham, for I will make you the father of many nations. I will make you extremely fruitful and will make nations and kings come from you. I will confirm my covenant that is between me and you and your future offspring throughout their generations. It is a permanent covenant to be your God and the God of your offspring after you. And to you and your future offspring I will give the land where you are residing—all the land of Canaan—as a permanent possession, and I will be their God."

Abraham's grandson, Jacob, was renamed Israel. God blessed the descendants of Abraham and Jacob. Hundreds of years later, the Israelites found themselves enslaved to the Pharaoh in Egypt. God raised up a deliverer for his people.

EXODUS 3:1-15

Moses was shepherding the flock of his father-in-law Jethro, the priest of Midian. He led the flock to the far side of the wilderness and came to Horeb, the mountain of God. Then the angel of the LORD appeared to him in a flame of fire within a bush. As Moses looked, he saw that the bush was on fire but was not consumed. So Moses thought, "I must go over and look at this remarkable sight. Why isn't the bush burning up?"

When the LORD saw that he had gone over to look, God called out to him from the bush, "Moses, Moses!"

"Here I am," he answered.

"Do not come closer," he said. "Remove the sandals from your feet, for the place where you are standing is holy ground." Then he continued, "I am the God of your father, the God of Abraham, the God of Isaac, and the God of Jacob." Moses hid his face because he was afraid to look at God.

Then the LORD said, "I have observed the misery of my people in Egypt, and have heard them crying out because of their oppressors. I know about their sufferings, and I have come down to rescue them from the power of the Egyptians and to bring them from that land to a good and spacious land, a land flowing with milk and honey—the territory of the Canaanites, Hethites, Amorites, Perizzites, Hivites, and Jebusites. So because the Israelites' cry for help has come to me, and I have also seen the way the Egyptians are oppressing them, therefore, go. I am sending you to Pharaoh so that you may lead my people, the Israelites, out of Egypt."

But Moses asked God, "Who am I that I should go to Pharaoh and that I should bring the Israelites out of Egypt?"

He answered, "I will certainly be with you, and this will be the sign to you that I am the one who sent you: when you bring the people out of Egypt, you will all worship God at this mountain."

Then Moses asked God, "If I go to the Israelites and say to them, 'The God of your fathers has sent me to you,' and they ask me, 'What is his name?' what should I tell them?"

God replied to Moses, "I AM WHO I AM. This is what you are to say to the Israelites: I AM has sent me to you." God also said to Moses, "Say this to the Israelites: The LORD, the God of your fathers, the God of Abraham, the God of Isaac, and the God of Jacob, has sent me to you. This is my name forever; this is how I am to be remembered in every generation.

God unleashed terrible plagues on Egypt, the last of which threatened the firstborn sons of all the land. At Passover, God provided a way for his people to be preserved from his judgment.

EXODUS 12:21-23,29-32

Moses summoned all the elders of Israel and said to them, "Go, select an animal from the flock according to your families, and slaughter the Passover animal. Take a cluster of hyssop, dip it in the blood that is in the basin, and brush the lintel and the two doorposts with some of the blood in the basin. None of you may go out the door of his house until morning. When the LORD passes through to strike Egypt and sees the blood on the lintel and the two doorposts, he will pass over the door and not let the destroyer enter your houses to strike you."

Now at midnight the LORD struck every firstborn male in the land of Egypt, from the firstborn of Pharaoh who sat on his throne to the firstborn of the prisoner who was in the dungeon, and every firstborn of the livestock. During the night Pharaoh got up, he along with all his officials and all the Egyptians, and there was a loud wailing throughout Egypt because there wasn't a house without someone dead. He summoned Moses and Aaron during the night and said, "Get out immediately from among my people, both you and the Israelites, and go, worship the LORD as you have said. Take even your flocks and your herds as you asked and leave, and also bless me."

After the Israelites escaped from Egypt, God
spoke to Moses on Mount Sinai and gave them
His Law, including the Ten Commandments.

EXODUS 19:3-6

Moses went up the mountain to God, and the LORD called to him from the mountain: "This is what you must say to the house of Jacob and explain to the Israelites: 'You have seen what I did to the Egyptians and how I carried you on eagles' wings and brought you to myself. Now if you will carefully listen to me and keep my covenant, you will be my own possession out of all the peoples, although the whole earth is mine, and you will be my kingdom of priests and my holy nation.' These are the words that you are to say to the Israelites."

EXODUS 20:1-17

God spoke all these words:
> I am the LORD your God, who brought you out
> of the land of Egypt, out of the place of slavery.
> Do not have other gods besides me.
> Do not make an idol for yourself, whether in
> the shape of anything in the heavens above

or on the earth below or in the waters under the earth. Do not bow in worship to them, and do not serve them; for I, the LORD your God, am a jealous God, punishing the children for the fathers' iniquity, to the third and fourth generations of those who hate me, but showing faithful love to a thousand generations of those who love me and keep my commands.

Do not misuse the name of the LORD your God, because the LORD will not leave anyone unpunished who misuses his name.

Remember the Sabbath day, to keep it holy: You are to labor six days and do all your work, but the seventh day is a Sabbath to the LORD your God. You must not do any work—you, your son or daughter, your male or female servant, your livestock, or the resident alien who is within your city gates. For the LORD made the heavens and the earth, the sea, and everything in them in six days; then he rested on the seventh day. Therefore the LORD blessed the Sabbath day and declared it holy.

Honor your father and your mother so that you may have a long life in the land that the LORD your God is giving you.

Do not murder.

Do not commit adultery.

Do not steal.

Do not give false testimony against your neighbor.

Do not covet your neighbor's house. Do not covet your neighbor's wife, his male

or female servant, his ox or donkey, or
anything that belongs to your neighbor.

*The Israelites rebelled against God and wandered
in the wilderness for more than forty years. In later
generations, the Israelites sung about the sins of
their ancestors and about the mercy of God.*

PSALM 78:1-8,17-39

My people, hear my instruction;
listen to the words from my mouth.
I will declare wise sayings;
I will speak mysteries from the past—
things we have heard and known
and that our fathers have passed down to us.
We will not hide them from their children,
but will tell a future generation
the praiseworthy acts of the LORD,
his might, and the wondrous works
he has performed.
He established a testimony in Jacob
and set up a law in Israel,
which he commanded our fathers
to teach to their children
so that a future generation—
children yet to be born—might know.
They were to rise and tell their children
so that they might put their confidence in God
and not forget God's works,

but keep his commands.
Then they would not be like their fathers,
a stubborn and rebellious generation,
a generation whose heart was not loyal
and whose spirit was not faithful to God.

They continued to sin against him,
rebelling in the desert against the Most High.
They deliberately tested God,
demanding the food they craved.
They spoke against God, saying,
"Is God able to provide food in the wilderness?
Look! He struck the rock and water gushed out;
torrents overflowed.
But can he also provide bread
or furnish meat for his people?"
Therefore, the LORD heard and became furious;
then fire broke out against Jacob,
and anger flared up against Israel
because they did not believe God
or rely on his salvation.
He gave a command to the clouds above
and opened the doors of heaven.
He rained manna for them to eat;
he gave them grain from heaven.
People ate the bread of angels.
He sent them an abundant supply of food.
He made the east wind blow in the skies
and drove the south wind by his might.
He rained meat on them like dust,
and winged birds like the sand of the seas.
He made them fall in the camp,
all around the tents.

The people ate and were completely satisfied,
for he gave them what they craved.
Before they had turned from what they craved,
while the food was still in their mouths,
God's anger flared up against them,
and he killed some of their best men.
He struck down Israel's fit young men.
Despite all this, they kept sinning
and did not believe his wondrous works.
He made their days end in futility,
their years in sudden disaster.
When he killed some of them,
the rest began to seek him;
they repented and searched for God.
They remembered that God was their rock,
the Most High God, their Redeemer.
But they deceived him with their mouths,
they lied to him with their tongues,
their hearts were insincere toward him,
and they were unfaithful to his covenant.
Yet he was compassionate;
he atoned for their iniquity
and did not destroy them.
He often turned his anger aside
and did not unleash all his wrath.
He remembered that they were only flesh,
a wind that passes and does not return.

*After Moses died, God raised up Joshua to lead
the Israelites into the land he had promised them.
But God continued to provide judges to deliver his
people because of their sin. Israel finally requested
a king to be like the surrounding nations.*

JOSHUA 1:1-9

After the death of Moses the LORD's servant,
the LORD spoke to Joshua son of Nun, Moses's assistant:
"Moses my servant is dead. Now you and all the people
prepare to cross over the Jordan to the land I am giving
the Israelites. I have given you every place where the
sole of your foot treads, just as I promised Moses. Your
territory will be from the wilderness and Lebanon to the
great river, the Euphrates River—all the land of the Hit-
tites—and west to the Mediterranean Sea. No one will
be able to stand against you as long as you live. I will be
with you, just as I was with Moses. I will not leave you or
abandon you.

"Be strong and courageous, for you will distribute
the land I swore to their fathers to give them as an inheritance. Above all, be strong and very courageous
to observe carefully the whole instruction my servant
Moses commanded you. Do not turn from it to the right
or the left, so that you will have success wherever you
go. This book of instruction must not depart from your
mouth; you are to meditate on it day and night so that you
may carefully observe everything written in it. For then
you will prosper and succeed in whatever you do. Haven't
I commanded you: be strong and courageous? Do not be

afraid or discouraged, for the Lord your God is with you wherever you go."

When Joshua had sent the people away, the Israelites had gone to take possession of the land, each to his own inheritance. The people worshiped the Lord throughout Joshua's lifetime and during the lifetimes of the elders who outlived Joshua. They had seen all the Lord's great works he had done for Israel.

Joshua son of Nun, the servant of the Lord, died at the age of 110. They buried him in the territory of his inheritance, in Timnath-heres, in the hill country of Ephraim, north of Mount Gaash. That whole generation was also gathered to their ancestors. After them another generation rose up who did not know the Lord or the works he had done for Israel.

The Israelites did what was evil in the Lord's sight. They worshiped the Baals and abandoned the Lord, the God of their fathers, who had brought them out of Egypt. They followed other gods from the surrounding peoples and bowed down to them. They angered the Lord, for they abandoned him and worshiped Baal and the Ashtoreths.

The Lord's anger burned against Israel, and he handed them over to marauders who raided them. He sold them to the enemies around them, and they could no longer resist their enemies. Whenever the Israelites went out, the Lord was against them and brought disaster on them, just as he had promised and sworn to them. So they suffered greatly.

The LORD raised up judges, who saved them from the power of their marauders, but they did not listen to their judges. Instead, they prostituted themselves with other gods, bowing down to them. They quickly turned from the way of their fathers, who had walked in obedience to the LORD's commands. They did not do as their fathers did. Whenever the LORD raised up a judge for the Israelites, the LORD was with him and saved the people from the power of their enemies while the judge was still alive. The LORD was moved to pity whenever they groaned because of those who were oppressing and afflicting them. Whenever the judge died, the Israelites would act even more corruptly than their fathers, following other gods to serve them and bow in worship to them. They did not turn from their evil practices or their obstinate ways.

1 SAMUEL 7:15–8:8

Samuel judged Israel throughout his life. Every year he would go on a circuit to Bethel, Gilgal, and Mizpah and would judge Israel at all these locations. Then he would return to Ramah because his home was there, he judged Israel there, and he built an altar to the LORD there.

When Samuel grew old, he appointed his sons as judges over Israel. His firstborn son's name was Joel and his second was Abijah. They were judges in Beer-sheba. However, his sons did not walk in his ways—they turned toward dishonest profit, took bribes, and perverted justice.

So all the elders of Israel gathered together and went to Samuel at Ramah. They said to him, "Look, you are old, and your sons do not walk in your ways. Therefore, appoint a king to judge us the same as all the other nations have."

When they said, "Give us a king to judge us," Samuel considered their demand wrong, so he prayed to the LORD. But the LORD told him, "Listen to the people and everything they say to you. They have not rejected you; they have rejected me as their king. They are doing the same thing to you that they have done to me, since the day I brought them out of Egypt until this day, abandoning me and worshiping other gods."

The first king of Israel, Saul, rejected God, and so the Lord sent Samuel to anoint another man as king.

1 SAMUEL 16:1B,6-13A

The LORD said to Samuel ... "Fill your horn with oil and go. I am sending you to Jesse of Bethlehem because I have selected a king from his sons."

When they arrived, Samuel saw Eliab and said, "Certainly the LORD's anointed one is here before him."

But the LORD said to Samuel, "Do not look at his appearance or his stature because I have rejected him. Humans do not see what the LORD sees, for humans see what is visible, but the LORD sees the heart."

Jesse called Abinadab and presented him to Samuel. "The LORD hasn't chosen this one either," Samuel said. Then Jesse presented Shammah, but Samuel said, "The LORD hasn't chosen this one either." After Jesse presented seven of his sons to him, Samuel told Jesse, "The LORD hasn't chosen any of these." Samuel asked him, "Are these all the sons you have?"

"There is still the youngest," he answered, "but right now he's tending the sheep." Samuel told Jesse, "Send for him. We won't sit down to eat until he gets here." So Jesse sent for him. He had beautiful eyes and a healthy, handsome appearance.

Then the LORD said, "Anoint him, for he is the one." So Samuel took the horn of oil and anointed him in the presence of his brothers, and the Spirit of the LORD came powerfully on David from that day forward.

God made a covenant with David, a king described as "a man after God's own heart."

2 SAMUEL 7:8-16

"This is what you are to say to my servant David: 'This is what the LORD of Armies says: I took you from the pasture, from tending the flock, to be ruler over my people Israel. I have been with you wherever you have gone, and I have destroyed all your enemies before you. I will make a great name for you like that of the greatest on the earth. I will designate a place for my people Israel and plant them, so that they may live there and not be disturbed again. Evildoers will not continue to oppress them as they have done ever since the day I ordered judges to be over my people Israel. I will give you rest from all your enemies.'"

"'The LORD declares to you: The LORD himself will make a house for you. When your time comes and you rest with your fathers, I will raise up after you your descendant, who will come from your body, and I will establish his kingdom. He is the one who will build a house for my name, and I will establish the throne of his kingdom forever. I will be his father, and he will be my son. When he does wrong, I will discipline him with a rod of men and blows from mortals. But my faithful love will never leave him as it did when I removed it from Saul, whom I removed from before you. Your house and kingdom will endure before me forever, and your throne will be established forever.'"

After the reign of David's son, Solomon, the kingdom of Israel was divided. Generations of kings followed. Some were faithful to the Lord, and others were not. Eventually, God judged the people by allowing other nations to conquer them.

2 CHRONICLES 36:15-23

The LORD, the God of their ancestors sent word against them by the hand of his messengers, sending them time and time again, for he had compassion on his people and on his dwelling place. But they kept ridiculing God's messengers, despising his words, and scoffing at his prophets, until the LORD's wrath was so stirred up against his people that there was no remedy. So he brought up against them the king of the Chaldeans, who killed their fit young men with the sword in the house of their sanctuary. He had no pity on young men or young women, elderly or aged; he handed them all over to him. He took everything to Babylon—all the articles of God's temple, large and small, the treasures of the LORD's temple, and the treasures of the king and his officials. Then the Chaldeans burned God's temple. They tore down Jerusalem's wall, burned all its palaces, and destroyed all its valuable articles.

He deported those who escaped from the sword to Babylon, and they became servants to him and his sons until the rise of the Persian kingdom. This fulfilled the word of the LORD through Jeremiah, and the land enjoyed its Sabbath rest all the days of the desolation until seventy years were fulfilled.

God preserved a remnant of his people, even in exile, and promised through the prophet Jeremiah to restore them to their land and establish a new covenant.

JEREMIAH 29:4-7,10-14

This is what the LORD of Armies, the God of Israel, says to all the exiles I deported from Jerusalem to Babylon: "Build houses and live in them. Plant gardens and eat their produce. Find wives for yourselves, and have sons and daughters. Find wives for your sons and give your daughters to men in marriage so that they may bear sons and daughters. Multiply there; do not decrease. Pursue the well-being of the city I have deported you to. Pray to the LORD on its behalf, for when it thrives, you will thrive."

For this is what the LORD says: "When seventy years for Babylon are complete, I will attend to you and will confirm my promise concerning you to restore you to this place. For I know the plans I have for you"—this is the LORD's declaration—"plans for your well-being, not for disaster, to give you a future and a hope. You will call to me and come and pray to me, and I will listen to you. You will seek me and find me when you search for me with all your heart. I will be found by you"—this is the LORD's declaration—"and I will restore your fortunes and gather you from all the nations and places where I banished you"—this is the LORD's declaration. "I will restore you to the place from which I deported you."

JEREMIAH 31:31-34

"Look, the days are coming"—this is the LORD's declaration—"when I will make a new covenant with the house of Israel and with the house of Judah. This one will not be like the covenant I made with their ancestors on the day I took them by the hand to lead them out of the land of Egypt—my covenant that they broke even though I am their master"—the LORD's declaration. "Instead, this is the covenant I will make with the house of Israel after those days"—the LORD's declaration. "I will put my teaching within them and write it on their hearts. I will be their God, and they will be my people. No longer will one teach his neighbor or his brother, saying, 'Know the LORD,' for they will all know me, from the least to the greatest of them"—this is the LORD's declaration. "For I will forgive their iniquity and never again remember their sin."

The prophets foretold a time when the Messiah would come to rescue God's people from exile. Hundreds of years before the time of Christ, Isaiah prophesied about a mysterious Servant, a man of suffering, who would take upon himself the sins of the people in order to bring about redemption.

ISAIAH 52:13–53:12

See, my servant will be successful;
he will be raised and lifted up
   and greatly exalted.
Just as many were appalled at you—
his appearance was so disfigured
that he did not look like a man,
and his form did not resemble
   a human being—
so he will sprinkle many nations.
Kings will shut their mouths because of him,
for they will see what had not been told them,
and they will understand what
   they had not heard.

Who has believed what we have heard?
And to whom has the arm of
   the Lord been revealed?
He grew up before him like a young plant
and like a root out of dry ground.
He didn't have an impressive form
or majesty that we should look at him,
no appearance that we should desire him.
He was despised and rejected by men,

a man of suffering who knew
    what sickness was.
He was like someone people turned
    away from;
he was despised, and we didn't value him.
Yet he himself bore our sicknesses,
and he carried our pains;
but we in turn regarded him stricken,
struck down by God, and afflicted.
But he was pierced because of our rebellion,
crushed because of our iniquities;
punishment for our peace was on him,
and we are healed by his wounds.
We all went astray like sheep;
we all have turned to our own way;
and the LORD has punished him
for the iniquity of us all.
He was oppressed and afflicted,
yet he did not open his mouth.
Like a lamb led to the slaughter
and like a sheep silent before her shearers,
he did not open his mouth.
He was taken away because of
    oppression and judgment;
and who considered his fate?
For he was cut off from the land of the living;
he was struck because of my people's rebellion.
He was assigned a grave with the wicked,
but he was with a rich man at his death,
because he had done no violence
and had not spoken deceitfully.
Yet the LORD was pleased to crush
    him severely.

When you make him a guilt offering,
he will see his seed, he will prolong his days,
and by his hand, the LORD's pleasure
    will be accomplished.
After his anguish,
he will see light and be satisfied.
By his knowledge,
my righteous servant will justify many,
and he will carry their iniquities.
Therefore I will give him the many as a portion,
and he will receive the mighty as spoil,
because he willingly submitted to death,
and was counted among the rebels;
yet he bore the sin of many
and interceded for the rebels.

*God's plan of redemption moves forward now in the
New Testament with the birth of Jesus Christ.*

LUKE 1:26-35,38

In the sixth month, the angel Gabriel was sent by God to
a town in Galilee called Nazareth, to a virgin engaged to
a man named Joseph, of the house of David. The virgin's
name was Mary. And the angel came to her and said,
"Greetings, favored woman! The Lord is with you." But
she was deeply troubled by this statement, wondering
what kind of greeting this could be. Then the angel told
her: "Do not be afraid, Mary, for you have found favor
with God. Now listen: You will conceive and give birth

to a son, and you will name him Jesus. He will be great and will be called the Son of the Most High, and the Lord God will give him the throne of his father David. He will reign over the house of Jacob forever, and his kingdom will have no end."

Mary asked the angel, "How can this be, since I have not had sexual relations with a man?"

The angel replied to her: "The Holy Spirit will come upon you, and the power of the Most High will overshadow you. Therefore, the holy one to be born will be called the Son of God.

"I am the Lord's servant," said Mary. "May it be done to me according to your word." Then the angel left her.

LUKE 2:1-7

In those days a decree went out from Caesar Augustus that the whole empire should be registered. This first registration took place while Quirinius was governing Syria. So everyone went to be registered, each to his own town.

Joseph also went up from the town of Nazareth in Galilee, to Judea, to the city of David, which is called Bethlehem, because he was of the house and family line of David, to be registered along with Mary, who was engaged to him and was pregnant. While they were there, the time came for her to give birth. Then she gave birth to her firstborn Son, and she wrapped him tightly in cloth and laid him in a manger, because there was no guest room available for them.

Jesus's ministry begins when he is baptized by John in the Jordan River, faces temptation in the wilderness, and then begins to proclaim the good news that God's kingdom has arrived.

MARK 1:9-20

In those days Jesus came from Nazareth in Galilee and was baptized in the Jordan by John. As soon as he came up out of the water, he saw the heavens being torn open and the Spirit descending on him like a dove. And a voice came from heaven: "You are my beloved Son; with you I am well-pleased."

Immediately the Spirit drove him into the wilderness. He was in the wilderness forty days, being tempted by Satan. He was with the wild animals, and the angels were serving him.

After John was arrested, Jesus went to Galilee, proclaiming the good news of God: "The time is fulfilled, and the kingdom of God has come near. Repent and believe the good news!"

As he passed alongside the Sea of Galilee, he saw Simon and Andrew, Simon's brother, casting a net into the sea—for they were fishermen. "Follow me," Jesus told them, "and I will make you fish for people." Immediately they left their nets and followed him. Going on a little farther, he saw James the son of Zebedee and his brother John in a boat putting their nets in order. Immediately he called them, and they left their father Zebedee in the boat with the hired men and followed him.

Jesus began to go all over Galilee, teaching in their synagogues, preaching the good news of the kingdom, and healing every disease and sickness among the people. Then the news about him spread throughout Syria. So they brought to him all those who were afflicted, those suffering from various diseases and intense pains, the demon-possessed, the epileptics, and the paralytics. And he healed them.

In addition to performing miracles, Jesus taught with authority and explained what the people of God are to be like and how they are to pray.

MATTHEW 5:3-12

"Blessed are the poor in spirit,
for the kingdom of heaven is theirs.
Blessed are those who mourn,
for they will be comforted.
Blessed are the humble,
for they will inherit the earth.
Blessed are those who hunger and
    thirst for righteousness,
for they will be filled.
Blessed are the merciful,
for they will be shown mercy.
Blessed are the pure in heart,
for they will see God.
Blessed are the peacemakers,

for they will be called sons of God.
Blessed are those who are persecuted
   because of righteousness,
for the kingdom of heaven is theirs.

"You are blessed when they insult you and persecute you and falsely say every kind of evil against you because of me. Be glad and rejoice, because your reward is great in heaven. For that is how they persecuted the prophets who were before you.

MATTHEW 6:9-13

"You should pray like this:
   Our Father in heaven,
   your name be honored as holy.
   Your kingdom come.
   Your will be done
   on earth as it is in heaven.
   Give us today our daily bread.
   And forgive us our debts,
   as we also have forgiven our debtors.
   And do not bring us into temptation,
   but deliver us from the evil one.

*Throughout the course of his ministry,
Jesus's identity as the long-promised Messiah
became clearer, and Jesus began to
predict his coming death.*

MATTHEW 16:13-21

When Jesus came to the region of Caesarea Philippi, he asked his disciples, "Who do people say that the Son of Man is?"

They replied, "Some say John the Baptist; others, Elijah; still others, Jeremiah or one of the prophets."

"But you," he asked them, "who do you say that I am?"

Simon Peter answered, "You are the Messiah, the Son of the living God."

Jesus responded, "Blessed are you, Simon son of Jonah, because flesh and blood did not reveal this to you, but my Father in heaven. And I also say to you that you are Peter, and on this rock I will build my church, and the gates of Hades will not overpower it. I will give you the keys of the kingdom of heaven, and whatever you bind on earth will have been bound in heaven, and whatever you loose on earth will have been loosed in heaven." Then he gave the disciples orders to tell no one that he was the Messiah.

From then on Jesus began to point out to his disciples that it was necessary for him to go to Jerusalem and suffer many things from the elders, chief priests, and scribes, be killed, and be raised the third day.

An expert in the law asked a question to test him: "Teacher, which command in the law is the greatest?"

He said to him, "Love the Lord your God with all your heart, with all your soul, and with all your mind. This is the greatest and most important command. The second is like it: Love your neighbor as yourself. All the Law and the Prophets depend on these two commands."

The plot against Jesus took shape during the Passover celebration. It was during this week that Jesus ate his last supper with his disciples.

MATTHEW 26:20-30

When evening came, he was reclining at the table with the Twelve. While they were eating, he said, "Truly I tell you, one of you will betray me."

Deeply distressed, each one began to say to him, "Surely not I, Lord?"

He replied, "The one who dipped his hand with me in the bowl—he will betray me. The Son of Man will go just as it is written about him, but woe to that man by whom the Son of Man is betrayed! It would have been better for him if he had not been born."

Judas, his betrayer, replied, "Surely not I, Rabbi?"

"You have said it," he told him.

As they were eating, Jesus took bread, blessed and broke it, gave it to the disciples, and said, "Take and eat it; this is my body." Then he took a cup, and after giving thanks, he gave it to them and said, "Drink from it, all of you. For this is my blood of the covenant, which is poured out for many for the forgiveness of sins. But I tell you, I will not drink from this fruit of the vine from now on until that day when I drink it new with you in my Father's kingdom." After singing a hymn, they went out to the Mount of Olives.

LUKE 22:39-48

He went out and made his way as usual to the Mount of Olives, and the disciples followed him. When he reached the place, he told them, "Pray that you may not fall into temptation." Then he withdrew from them about a stone's throw, knelt down, and began to pray, "Father, if you are willing, take this cup away from me—nevertheless, not my will, but yours, be done."

Then an angel from heaven appeared to him, strengthening him. Being in anguish, he prayed more fervently, and his sweat became like drops of blood falling to the ground. When he got up from prayer and came to the disciples, he found them sleeping, exhausted from their grief. "Why are you sleeping?" he asked them. "Get up and pray, so that you won't fall into temptation."

While he was still speaking, suddenly a mob came, and one of the Twelve named Judas was leading them. He came near Jesus to kiss him, but Jesus said to him, "Judas, are you betraying the Son of Man with a kiss?"

Jesus endured a series of mock trials that ended up with him standing before Pilate, the Roman ruler of the area.

Pilate came out to them and said, "What charge do you bring against this man?"

They answered him, "If this man weren't a criminal, we wouldn't have handed him over to you."

Pilate told them, "You take him and judge him according to your law."

"It's not legal for us to put anyone to death," the Jews declared. They said this so that Jesus's words might be fulfilled indicating what kind of death he was going to die.

Then Pilate went back into the headquarters, summoned Jesus, and said to him, "Are you the King of the Jews?"

Jesus answered, "Are you asking this on your own, or have others told you about me?"

"I'm not a Jew, am I?" Pilate replied. "Your own nation and the chief priests handed you over to me. What have you done?"

"My kingdom is not of this world," said Jesus. "If my kingdom were of this world, my servants would fight, so that I wouldn't be handed over to the Jews. But as it is, my kingdom is not from here."

"You are a king then?" Pilate asked.

"You say that I'm a king," Jesus replied. "I was born for this, and I have come into the world for this: to testify to the truth. Everyone who is of the truth listens to my voice."

"What is truth?" said Pilate.

After he had said this, he went out to the Jews again and told them, "I find no grounds for charging him. You have a custom that I release one prisoner to you at the Passover. So, do you want me to release to you the King of the Jews?"

They shouted back, "Not this man, but Barabbas!" Now Barabbas was a revolutionary.

Then Pilate took Jesus and had him flogged. The soldiers also twisted together a crown of thorns, put it on his head, and clothed him in a purple robe. And they kept coming up to him and saying, "Hail, King of the Jews!" and were slapping his face.

Pilate went outside again and said to them, "Look, I'm bringing him out to you to let you know I find no grounds for charging him." Then Jesus came out wearing the crown of thorns and the purple robe. Pilate said to them, "Here is the man!"

When the chief priests and the temple servants saw him, they shouted, "Crucify! Crucify!"

Pilate responded, "Take him and crucify him yourselves, since I find no grounds for charging him."

"We have a law," the Jews replied to him, "and according to that law he ought to die, because he made himself the Son of God."

When Pilate heard this statement, he was more afraid than ever. He went back into the headquarters and asked Jesus, "Where are you from?" But Jesus did not give him an answer. So Pilate said to him, "Do you refuse to speak to me? Don't you know that I have the authority to release you and the authority to crucify you?"

"You would have no authority over me at all," Jesus answered him, "if it hadn't been given you from above. This is why the one who handed me over to you has the greater sin."

From that moment Pilate kept trying to release him. But the Jews shouted, "If you release this man, you are not Caesar's friend. Anyone who makes himself a king opposes Caesar!"

When Pilate heard these words, he brought Jesus outside. He sat down on the judge's seat in a place called the Stone Pavement (but in Aramaic, *Gabbatha*). It was the preparation day for the Passover, and it was about noon. Then he told the Jews, "Here is your king!"

They shouted, "Take him away! Take him away! Crucify him!"

Pilate said to them, "Should I crucify your king?"

"We have no king but Caesar!" the chief priests answered.

Then he handed him over to be crucified.

Once sentenced to death, Jesus was led to Golgotha, the place of his execution.

LUKE 23:32-56

Two others—criminals—were also led away to be executed with him. When they arrived at the place called The Skull, they crucified him there, along with the criminals, one on the right and one on the left. Then Jesus said, "Father, forgive them, because they do not know what they are doing." And they divided his clothes and cast lots.

The people stood watching, and even the leaders were scoffing: "He saved others; let him save himself if this is God's Messiah, the Chosen One!" The soldiers also mocked him. They came offering him sour wine and said, "If you are the King of the Jews, save yourself!"

An inscription was above him: THIS IS THE KING OF THE JEWS.

Then one of the criminals hanging there began to yell insults at him: "Aren't you the Messiah? Save yourself and us!"

But the other answered, rebuking him: "Don't you even fear God, since you are undergoing the same punishment? We are punished justly, because we're getting back what we deserve for the things we did, but this man has done nothing wrong." Then he said, "Jesus, remember me when you come into your kingdom."

And he said to him, "Truly I tell you, today you will be with me in paradise."

It was now about noon, and darkness came over the whole land until three, because the sun's light failed. The curtain of the sanctuary was split down the middle. And Jesus called out with a loud voice, "Father, into your hands I entrust my spirit." Saying this, he breathed his last.

When the centurion saw what happened, he began to glorify God, saying, "This man really was righteous!" All the crowds that had gathered for this spectacle, when they saw what had taken place, went home, striking their chests. But all who knew him, including the women who had followed him from Galilee, stood at a distance, watching these things.

There was a good and righteous man named Joseph, a member of the Sanhedrin, who had not agreed with their plan and action. He was from Arimathea, a Judean town, and was looking forward to the kingdom of God. He approached Pilate and asked for Jesus's body. Taking it down, he wrapped it in fine linen and placed it in a tomb cut into the rock, where no one had ever been placed. It was the preparation day, and the Sabbath was about to begin. The women who had come with him from Galilee followed along and observed the tomb and how his body was placed. Then they returned and prepared spices and perfumes. And they rested on the Sabbath according to the commandment.

LUKE 24:1-12,36-53

On the first day of the week, very early in the morning, they came to the tomb, bringing the spices they had prepared.

They found the stone rolled away from the tomb. They went in but did not find the body of the Lord Jesus. While they were perplexed about this, suddenly two men stood by them in dazzling clothes. So the women were terrified and bowed down to the ground. "Why are you looking for the living among the dead?" asked the men. "He is not here, but he has risen! Remember how he spoke to you when he was still in Galilee, saying, 'It is necessary that the Son of Man be betrayed into the hands of sinful men, be crucified, and rise on the third day'?" And they remembered his words.

Returning from the tomb, they reported all these things to the Eleven and to all the rest. Mary Magdalene, Joanna, Mary the mother of James, and the other women with them were telling the apostles these things. But these words seemed like nonsense to them, and they did not believe the women. Peter, however, got up and ran to the tomb. When he stooped to look in, he saw only the linen cloths. So he went away, amazed at what had happened.

As they were saying these things, he himself stood in their midst. He said to them, "Peace to you!" But they were startled and terrified and thought they were seeing a ghost. "Why are you troubled?" he asked them. "And why do doubts arise in your hearts? Look at my hands and my feet, that it is I myself! Touch me and see, because a ghost does not have flesh and bones as you can see I have." Having said this, he showed them his hands and feet. But while they still were amazed and in disbelief because of their joy, he asked them, "Do you have anything here to eat?" So they gave him a piece of a broiled fish, and he took it and ate in their presence.

He told them, "These are my words that I spoke to you while I was still with you—that everything written about me in the Law of Moses, the Prophets, and the Psalms must be fulfilled." Then he opened their minds to understand the Scriptures. He also said to them, "This is what is written: The Messiah would suffer and rise from the dead the third day, and repentance for forgiveness of sins would be proclaimed in his name to all the nations, beginning at Jerusalem. You are witnesses of these things. And look, I am sending you what my Father promised. As for you, stay in the city until you are empowered from on high."

Then he led them out to the vicinity of Bethany, and lifting up his hands he blessed them. And while he was blessing them, he left them and was carried up into heaven. After worshiping him, they returned to Jerusalem with great joy. And they were continually in the temple praising God.

About ten days after Jesus ascended into heaven,
the Holy Spirit came with power upon the disciples,
so that they were able to preach the gospel.

ACTS 2

When the day of Pentecost had arrived, they were all together in one place. Suddenly a sound like that of a violent rushing wind came from heaven, and it filled the whole house where they were staying. They saw tongues like flames of fire that separated and rested on each one of them. Then they were all filled with the Holy Spirit and began to speak in different tongues, as the Spirit enabled them.

Now there were Jews staying in Jerusalem, devout people from every nation under heaven. When this sound occurred, a crowd came together and was confused because each one heard them speaking in his own language. They were astounded and amazed, saying, "Look, aren't all these who are speaking Galileans? How is it that each of us can hear them in our own native language? Parthians, Medes, Elamites; those who live in Mesopotamia, in Judea and Cappadocia, Pontus and Asia, Phrygia and Pamphylia, Egypt and the parts of Libya near Cyrene; visitors from Rome (both Jews and converts), Cretans and Arabs—we hear them declaring the magnificent acts of God in our own tongues." They were all astounded and perplexed, saying to one another, "What does this mean?" But some sneered and said, "They're drunk on new wine."

Peter stood up with the Eleven, raised his voice, and proclaimed to them: "Fellow Jews and all you residents of

Jerusalem, let me explain this to you and pay attention to my words. For these people are not drunk, as you suppose, since it's only nine in the morning. On the contrary, this is what was spoken through the prophet Joel:

> And it will be in the last days, says God,
> that I will pour out my Spirit on all people;
> then your sons and your
>   daughters will prophesy,
> your young men will see visions,
> and your old men will dream dreams.
> I will even pour out my Spirit
> on my servants in those days,
>   both men and women
> and they will prophesy.
> I will display wonders in the heaven above
> and signs on the earth below:
> blood and fire and a cloud of smoke.
> The sun will be turned to darkness
> and the moon to blood
> before the great and glorious
>   day of the Lord comes.
> Then everyone who calls
> on the name of the Lord will be saved.

"Fellow Israelites, listen to these words: This Jesus of Nazareth was a man attested to you by God with miracles, wonders, and signs that God did among you through him, just as you yourselves know. Though he was delivered up according to God's determined plan and foreknowledge, you used lawless people to nail him to a cross and kill him. God raised him up, ending the pains of death, because it was not possible for him to be held by death. For David says of him:

I saw the Lord ever before me;
because he is at my right hand,
I will not be shaken.
Therefore my heart is glad
and my tongue rejoices.
Moreover, my flesh will rest in hope,
because you will not abandon me in Hades
or allow your holy one to see decay.
You have revealed the paths of life to me;
you will fill me with gladness
in your presence.

"Brothers and sisters, I can confidently speak to you about the patriarch David: He is both dead and buried, and his tomb is with us to this day. Since he was a prophet, he knew that God had sworn an oath to him to seat one of his descendants on his throne. Seeing what was to come, he spoke concerning the resurrection of the Messiah: He was not abandoned in Hades, and his flesh did not experience decay.

"God has raised this Jesus; we are all witnesses of this. Therefore, since he has been exalted to the right hand of God and has received from the Father the promised Holy Spirit, he has poured out what you both see and hear. For it was not David who ascended into the heavens, but he himself says:

The Lord declared to my Lord,
'Sit at my right hand
until I make your enemies your footstool.'

"Therefore let all the house of Israel know with certainty that God has made this Jesus, whom you crucified, both Lord and Messiah."

When they heard this, they were pierced to the heart and said to Peter and the rest of the apostles: "Brothers, what should we do?"

Peter replied, "Repent and be baptized, each of you, in the name of Jesus Christ for the forgiveness of your sins, and you will receive the gift of the Holy Spirit. For the promise is for you and for your children, and for all who are far off,as many as the Lord our God will call." With many other words he testified and strongly urged them, saying, "Be saved from this corrupt generation!" So those who accepted his message were baptized, and that day about three thousand people were added to them.

They devoted themselves to the apostles' teaching, to the fellowship, to the breaking of bread, and to prayer.

Everyone was filled with awe, and many wonders and signs were being performed through the apostles. Now all the believers were together and held all things in common. They sold their possessions and property and distributed the proceeds to all, as any had need. Every day they devoted themselves to meeting together in the temple, and broke bread from house to house. They ate their food with joyful and sincere hearts, praising God and enjoying the favor of all the people. Every day the Lord added to their number those who were being saved.

A persecutor of the early Christians, Paul, encountered the risen Jesus on the road to Damascus. More than anyone else in the first century, Paul helped to spread the gospel to Jews and Gentiles alike, proclaiming that the crucified and risen Jesus was the Messiah of Israel and Lord of the whole world. He wrote many letters in which he explained the meaning of Jesus's death and resurrection to the early Christians.

ROMANS 3:21-26

Now, apart from the law, the righteousness of God has been revealed, attested by the Law and the Prophets. The righteousness of God is through faith in Jesus Christ to all who believe, since there is no distinction. For all have sinned and fall short of the glory of God. They are justified freely by his grace through the redemption that is in Christ Jesus. God presented him as an atoning sacrifice in his blood, received through faith, to demonstrate his righteousness, because in his restraint God passed over the sins previously committed. God presented him to demonstrate his righteousness at the present time, so that he would be righteous and declare righteous the one who has faith in Jesus.

ROMANS 10:8B-13

This is the message of faith that we proclaim: If you confess with your mouth, "Jesus is Lord," and believe in your heart that God raised him from the dead, you will be saved. One believes with the heart, resulting in righteousness, and one confesses with the mouth, resulting in salvation. For the Scripture says, Everyone who believes on him will not be put to shame, since there is no distinction between Jew and Greek, because the same Lord of all richly blesses all who call on him. For everyone who calls on the name of the Lord will be saved.

EPHESIANS 2:1-10,13-22

You were dead in your trespasses and sins in which you previously lived according to the ways of this world, according to the ruler of the power of the air, the spirit now working in the disobedient. We too all previously lived among them in our fleshly desires, carrying out the inclinations of our flesh and thoughts, and we were by nature children under wrath as the others were also. But God, who is rich in mercy, because of his great love that he had for us, made us alive with Christ even though we were dead in trespasses. You are saved by grace! He also raised us up with him and seated us with him in the heavens in Christ Jesus, so that in the coming ages he might display the immeasurable riches of his grace through his kindness to us in Christ Jesus. For you are saved by grace through faith, and this is not from yourselves; it is God's gift— not from works, so that no one can boast. For we are his workmanship, created in Christ Jesus for good works, which God prepared ahead of time for us to do.

But now in Christ Jesus, you who were far away have been brought near by the blood of Christ. For he is our peace, who made both groups one and tore down the dividing wall of hostility. In his flesh, he made of no effect the law consisting of commands and expressed in regulations, so that he might create in himself one new man from the two, resulting in peace. He did this so that he might reconcile both to God in one body through the cross by which he put the hostility to death. He came and proclaimed the good news of peace to you who were far away and peace to those who were near. For through him we both have access in one spirit to the Father. So then you are no longer foreigners and strangers, but fellow citizens with the saints, and members of God's household, built on the foundation of the apostles and prophets, with Christ Jesus himself as the cornerstone. In him the whole building, being put together, grows into a holy temple in the Lord. In him you are also being built together for God's dwelling in the Spirit.

The last book of the Bible records a vision of John—a description of the final restoration of the world that God has promised to bring about.

REVELATION 21:1-8

I saw a new heaven and a new earth; for the first heaven and the first earth had passed away, and the sea was no more. I also saw the holy city, the new Jerusalem, coming down out of heaven from God, prepared like a bride adorned for her husband.

Then I heard a loud voice from the throne: Look, God's dwelling is with humanity, and he will live with them. They will be his peoples, and God himself will be with them and will be their God. He will wipe away every tear from their eyes. Death will be no more; grief, crying, and pain will be no more, because the previous things have passed away.

Then the one seated on the throne said, "Look, I am making everything new." He also said, "Write, because these words are faithful and true." Then he said to me, "It is done! I am the Alpha and the Omega, the beginning and the end. I will freely give to the thirsty from the spring of the water of life. The one who conquers will inherit these things, and I will be his God, and he will be my son. But the cowards, faithless, detestable, murderers, sexually immoral, sorcerers, idolaters, and all liars—their share will be in the lake that burns with fire and sulfur, which is the second death."

REVELATION 22:16-17,20-21

"I, Jesus, have sent my angel to attest these things to you for the churches. I am the root and descendant of David, the bright morning star."

Both the Spirit and the bride say, "Come!" Let anyone who hears, say, "Come!" Let the one who is thirsty come. Let the one who desires take the water of life freely.

He who testifies about these things says, "Yes, I am coming soon."

Amen! Come, Lord Jesus!

The grace of the Lord Jesus be with everyone. Amen.

NOTES

NOTES

NOTES

NOTES